THE GOLDEN THREAD

A SONG FOR PETE SEEGER

By
COLIN MELOY

Illustrated by
NIKKI McCLURE

BALZER + BRAY
An Imprint of HarperCollins Publishers

THE GOLDEN THREAD

I heard there was a golden thread
  A shining, magic thing
That bounded up our little world
  –I HEARD PETE SEEGER SING!

PETE!
PETE!

What rhymes with Pete?

A miner's cleat, a fishing fleet, the sound of
many marching feet—
To hear Pete Seeger sing!

Was it a song that I heard sung
  Along a cobbled alley?
Or from a merry sailing sloop
  That plied the Hudson River Valley?

HAMMER BRINGER!
RIVER SINGER!
SAILOR, SOLDIER,
LEAN BELL RINGER

A fighter in peace, musician in war

    He followed that string till he couldn't no more

But before we get this string a-singing

All strings must have their first beginning. . . .

Pete was raised by musical hands

The third-born member of a family band!

Playing twelve-night stands

ALL HANDS!
ALL HANDS!

Bringing Bach to backwaters

Packing sons and daughters

In a Model T Ford

With the boys on the boards

And a bucket to wash all the diapers

GO TELL AUNT RHODY THE OLD GREY GOO

And our Pete grew

   He grew and grew

      Ten stories high, it might seem to you

Let's give him a banjo, slung over his shoulder

Let's give him a song, let's make him a soldier

In World War Two

   —What's a pacifist to do?

Armed with a banjo, he followed along

To keep soldiers in cheer by singing 'em songs

A banjo can do more good than a gun

    And it's a lot more fun, as there are songs to be sung

    And chords to be wrung

    And voices to be brung 'round in harmony

OH, PETE, PETE

When next we meet
We find you on a brimming street
The crowds, they're reaching
    mountain-size
And you're teaching folks to

ORGANIZE!
UNIONIZE!

Preaching workers' rights to picket lines
At factories, farms, in copper mines

And speaking of union . . .

By now our Pete's a married man
That thread twines 'round the two right hands
Of Pete and Toshi-Aline Ohta
This love song wouldn't reach its coda
Till years had flown, and children grown
(Whom Toshi often raised alone
While Pete a-rambled far from home)

UND THAT RING WHEN YOU MEET YOUR NEW PARTNER GIVE HER A SWING!

And what to do with golden thread

But keep spinning it, hymning it

Till it's worldwide spread—that's what Pete did.

He took a song called "I'll Be All Right"

That he heard sung for the labor fight

And he changed it around for a new crowd to hum
To proudly pronounce: "We Shall Overcome."
(This beautiful song, with Pete's humble improvement,
became a great anthem for the civil rights movement.)

GOODNIGHT, IRENE

But like every God needs its own believers

Don't every thread need its own Weavers?

A bold ensemble to sing and praise!

Ronnie, Fred, and the great Lee Hays

(A friend from Pete's old picketing days)

They sang out songs both wild and serene

They gave the world its "Goodnight Irene"

Which topped the charts for twenty-five weeks

A WORLDWIDE SMASH!
A NUMBER-ONE PEAK!

THE FASCISTS CAME WITH

But now our story takes a darker turn

(Like every season must turn, turn, turn)

For at this time, a Cold War burned

And it seemed that our country had quite lost its way

When fear and oppression began to hold sway

TO PRISON US IN HATE

CHAINS AND WAR

Folks were suspected for things they believed
  For the thoughts that they carried
  For the threads that they weaved . . .
See, Pete sang for anyone: by day or by night,

Be they **CAPIT'LIST,**
COMMUNIST,
on left or on right

AND MANY A GOOD MAN FOUGHT

PEOPLE'S
SONGS
TONITE
UNITE

Our Pete found himself quite caught up in this mess

For not caring a tick 'bout which folks he addressed

   Or for whom he had sung

   And when all's said and done

Pete was then sent to a senator's court

And thereupon angrily asked to report

   About all his doings and political leanings

   And did any of his songs have nefarious meanings?

All this just to settle political scores

But Pete, he just said: "It's no business of yours."

WHICH IT WASN'T!
STILL ISN'T!

It's our right to free speech

     Without fear of reprisal, beyond government reach

Pete was a patriot, was right to resist

   But for all of his troubles, he was put on a BLACKLIST

    And they blackened his name

    And they dampened his flame

    And insisted that everyone look on in shame

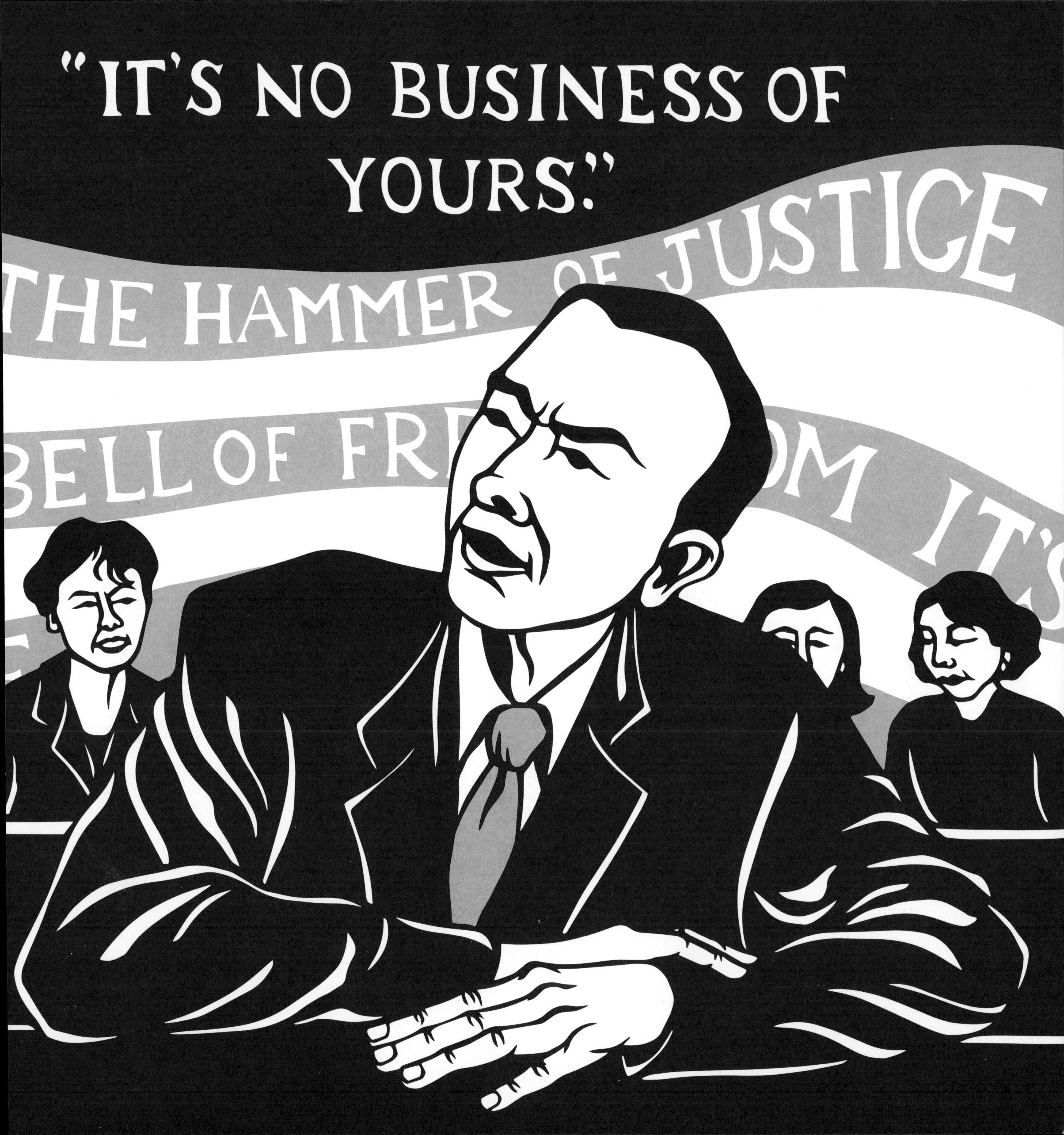
"IT'S NO BUSINESS OF YOURS."
THE HAMMER
JUSTICE
BELL OF FR
OM IT'S

BUT DID THIS STOP OUR HERO PETE SEEGER?
NO!

He kept playing music, he kept playing songs

He traveled the world with his fam'ly along

With his banjo in tow

Playing show after show

Pete followed that thread and its long, golden glow

But despite these adventures, and the places they took him
Back in the US, they still wouldn't book him
On TV or concerts or radio shows
Pete just had to make it all work on his own

His voice kept on ringing in song
As long as folks sang right along

And after a time, those voices got louder
Stronger and bolder, poetic and vital
With Dylan and Baez, Ochs and Odetta—
and Pete at the forefront—

—IT WAS A REVIVAL!

A festival forged on the shores of New England
In Newport, Rhode Island, these folk found a home
And Pete was the plowman, on spade and on furrow
And music's sound seedlings found this fertile loam

This thread was a lifeline, a tuneful gift giver
A thing that entwines us, a deep winding river

FINE I'D WEAVE A MAGIC STRAND OF RAINBOW DESIGN

A river that bounded the house that he made
On the hills of the highlands, in a wide wooded glade
Hand hewn and rough hewn, timbered and tall
He built with his hands all these high wooded walls
And up in this homestead, Pete whiled away times
   Out chopping old wood and pairing up rhymes
But that river! The Hudson! All mired in its glop
Who knows what would happen if you just drank a drop
(A swimmer should think twice to take just one lap in)
Well, Pete, good old Pete, COULD NOT let this happen

So he built him a ship! A fine wooden sloop
    To spread the good word on the Hudson's vile soup
The *Clearwater* sailed from New York to Beacon
    Albany, Annandale, land of Mohicans!

        Like voices harmonious and joined in a song,
        Folks helped make that river flow cleanly and strong

As threads have beginnings

So must they have ends

Just like a river in its bows and its bends

As it starts in the mountains and flows to the sea

It spreads the world over when it fin'lly breaks free

AND A TIME TO EVERY PURPOSE

Pete's thread stretched long, it bridged generations
Through Depressions, Recessions, and high celebrations
He followed it doggedly, and with all of his heart
He wove it and drove it into his own art

Now Pete is beyond us, he's passed on away
But his legacy still surrounds us today
In music, in rivers, in organization
A hero to all in this young mighty nation

ONE EARTH SO GREEN AND

WHO COULD ASK FOR

Oh, I heard there was a golden thread

A shining magic thing

That bounded up our little imperfect world

I HEARD PETE SEEGER SING.

NOBODY LIVING CAN EVER

THIS LAND WAS MADE

May 3, 1919—Pete is born in New York City to a pair of teaching musicians, Charlie and Constance Seeger. When Pete is little, his father brings him and his brothers on a tour of rural New York, playing classical music for working folk.

1927—Pete learns his first instrument, the ukulele, at age eight. His true love, however, ends up being the five-string banjo, which he plays in the clawhammer style.

1936—Pete's two brothers, John and Charles, chip in to help pay for Pete's tuition at Harvard University. Pete gets to playing in folk clubs and at square dances. Consequently, his grades fall. He drops out of college to pursue a career in music.

1941—Pete forms a group called the Almanac Singers, which eventually boasts Woody Guthrie as a member. They perform at union rallies around the country.

1942—At the advent of the US involvement in World War Two, Pete is drafted into the army. He doesn't, however, end up fighting in the war; instead, he is conscripted to play banjo for injured servicemen and organize theatrical events at an army hospital.

1943—Pete marries Toshi-Aline Ohta, a woman he'd met at a square dance. Theirs is to be a marriage that would last both of their lifetimes.

1948—Upon returning home from service, Pete forms the Weavers with singer Lee Hays, singer Ronnie Gilbert, and singer-guitarist Fred Hellerman.

1951—The Weavers release a version of Leadbelly's tune "Goodnight Irene," which becomes a sensation, topping the Billboard charts for thirteen weeks.

1955—Pete is targeted by the House Un-American Activities Committee, or HUAC, for having ties to the Communist Party. He refuses to testify against himself, insisting that he had a constitutional right to privacy and the committee had no business digging into his affairs.

1957—After a protracted trial, Pete is blacklisted. Many bookers of clubs, TV shows, and radio programs are afraid to book him in concert for fear of the controversy.

Pete spends much of the fifties playing in schoolrooms and on college campuses. He and Toshi had built a log house on their property near Beacon, New York, and there they raise their children Daniel, Tinya, and Mika. (Their first child, Peter, died in his infancy.)

1959—Pete helps found the Newport Folk Festival in Newport, Rhode Island. It becomes a gathering place for some of the brighter luminaries of the American folk revival: Bob Dylan, Joan Baez, Odetta, Phil Ochs, and Judy Collins (to name a very few). All the while, Pete tours the world playing his banjo, singing and leading audiences in song.

1966—Pete and Toshi help found the Clearwater Festival, to raise awareness of the polluted state of the Hudson River.

1969—The Smothers Brothers effectively end the blacklisting of Pete Seeger when they invite him on their TV variety show. Also in this year, Pete helps build the sloop *Clearwater*, a wooden sailing vessel, to ply the waters of the Hudson. The ship becomes a powerful tool for raising awareness of the unhealthy state of the river. An organization springs up around the festival and the ship, which spearheads the push to clean up the river and make it safe for humans and wildlife alike.

1980—The Weavers reunite for a concert at Carnegie Hall.

1996—Pete is inducted into the Rock and Roll Hall of Fame.

2001—Pete is the recipient of a Kennedy Center Honor.

2008—Pete once more leads the country in song, singing Woody Guthrie's tune "This Land Is Your Land" in a nationally broadcast concert in celebration of President Barack Obama's inauguration.

2013—Toshi-Aline Seeger dies.

January 27, 2014—Pete Seeger dies in New York City, age 94.

Pete Seeger was an American activist, performer, guitar player, banjo player, singer, songwriter, sailor, woodchopper, environmentalist, carpenter, and boatbuilder. In his life, Pete wrote or arranged some of the more important American songs of his day: "Turn, Turn, Turn"; "We Shall Overcome"; "Where Have All the Flowers Gone?"; and "Deep Muddy"—a scant selection from the hundreds of songs he wrote or arranged. He is remembered as a great patriot, a seminal leader and singer of songs, and a fighter for the oppressed and marginalized peoples of the world.

RECOMMENDED LISTENING

With the Almanac Singers

Songs for John Doe (1941)

Talking Union (1955)

With the Weavers

The Weavers at Carnegie Hall (1957)

Greatest Hits (1957)

The Reunion at Carnegie Hall (1963)

As Pete Seeger

American Folk Songs for Children (1954)

Goofing-Off Suite (1955)

American Industrial Ballads (1956)

The Rainbow Quest (1960)

Songs of the Spanish Civil War, Vol. 1 (1961)

Children's Concert at Town Hall (1963)

Waist Deep in the Big Muddy
and Other Love Songs (1967)

Abiyoyo and Other Story Songs for Children (1967)

Rainbow Race (1971)

Singalong Demonstration Concert (1980)

Live at Newport (1993)

Pete Seeger at 89 (2008)

Anthologies/Compilations

If I Had a Hammer: Songs of Hope and Struggle (1998)

American Favorite Ballads, Volumes 1–5 (2009)

AUTHOR'S NOTE

Even though I only met him once, briefly, in 2011, it really feels like Pete Seeger has been a lifelong acquaintance of mine. He was there in the songs my family sang around campfires; he was there, smiling and singing, on the LP sleeves on my parents' record shelves. He showed up in photographs of civil rights marches and union rallies; his voice was an undeniable presence in the modern environmental movement. I admit to having wept with patriotic pride listening to him, over the radio, lead the crowd singing "This Land Is Your Land" at the Lincoln Memorial in 2009. My admiration for him has only grown, researching and writing the simple verse for this book. I'd like to thank Donna Bray for giving me the opportunity to celebrate Pete's life this way and to Tao Rodriguez Seeger for, early on in the writing process, providing illuminating perspective on his incredible grandfather.

ARTIST'S NOTE

The time of making matters. Pete Seeger sang through key moments in America's history. Pete was there. The history of his life is American history. These images were made during the fall of 2016 and the winter of 2017. Pete was there with me as history was being made. I played his *Rainbow Quest* television shows while I worked. Pete's voice and cadence, his long limbs and smiles, all his songs and friends kept me company and gave me courage and strength to make.

  To illustrate Pete's life, I spent hours watching videos of him playing and talking. As I watched, I sketched and took pictures to use for his expressions. Pete always seemed happiest when he stepped away from his mike and the crowd sang strong. I listened to his songs and sang as loud as I could and harmonized when I could find the right notes. I compiled historical photos of boats, people, signs, factories, and hats and tried to keep track of banjo frets. All the images are cut from paper using an X-Acto knife. Two layers were cut, a black layer and a gold layer.

  Thank you, Colin, for this work, and thanks, Carson, for encouraging me to pick up the thread and illustrate this song. Thank you, Donna Bray, for being open to this possibility, and to Steven Malk for opportunities to share. Thank you, Susan, for allowing me to pause work to seize this moment, and Scott, for pausing his. And finally, thanks to Jay T. and Finn, my family, for singing albums of songs on long car rides across this land.

  This book is an act of remembering but also of looking forward. What history will we be part of? What will this time make? Listen and share.

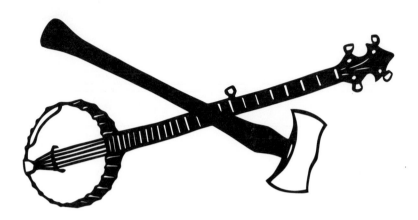

BIBLIOGRAPHY

Seeger, Pete. *Where Have All the Flowers Gone: A Singalong Memoir.* New York: W. W. Norton & Company, 2009.

Wilkinson, Alec. *The Protest Singer: An Intimate Portrait of Pete Seeger.* New York: Alfred A. Knopf, 2009.

Songs quoted in the art: pp. 6–7: "This Land Is Your Land" by Woody Guthrie; **p. 9: "We Shall Not Be Moved" (American folk song), "Skip to My Lou" (children's song), "Union Maid" by Woody Guthrie, "Leave Her, Johnny" (traditional sea chantey), and "Bourgeois Blues" by Lead Belly;** p. 11: "If I Had a Hammer" by Pete Seeger and Lee Hays; **p. 13: "Go Tell Aunt Rhody" (American folk song);** p. 15: "Strange Death of John Doe" by Millard Lampell; **pp. 16–17: "Talking Union" by Lee Hays, Millard Lampell, and Pete Seeger;** pp. 18–19: old-time square-dance call; **pp. 20–21: "We Shall Overcome" (American gospel song) adapted by Pete Seeger;** pp. 22–23: "Goodnight, Irene" by Lead Belly; **pp. 24–25: "Wasn't That a Time?" by Lee Hays and Walter Lowenfels;** pp. 26–27: "If I Had a Hammer" by Pete Seeger and Lee Hays; **p. 29: Taiko drum chant;** p. 31: "Froggy Went A-Courtin'" (Scottish folk song); **pp. 32–33: "Oh, Had I a Golden Thread" by Pete Seeger;** p. 35: "My Dirty Stream (The Hudson River Song)" by Pete Seeger; **p. 36: "Sailing down My Golden River" by Pete Seeger;** pp. 38–39: "Turn! Turn! Turn!" by Pete Seeger; **pp. 40–41: "My Rainbow Race" (American folk and children's song);** pp. 42–43: "This Land Is Your Land" by Woody Guthrie

Balzer + Bray is an imprint of HarperCollins Publishers.

The Golden Thread: A Song for Pete Seeger
Text copyright © 2018 by Unadoptable Books LLC
Illustrations copyright © 2018 by Nikki McClure
All rights reserved. Manufactured in China.
No part of this book may be used or reproduced in any manner whatsoever without written permission except in the case of brief quotations embodied in critical articles and reviews. For information address HarperCollins Children's Books, a division of HarperCollins Publishers, 195 Broadway, New York, NY 10007.
www.harpercollinschildrens.com

Library of Congress Control Number: 2016941964
ISBN 978-0-06-236825-6

The artist took her own photos of Pete from filmed performances and used historical photos to make the images. Artwork was created by cutting black paper with an X-Acto knife. Golden paper was cut for additional layers of songs and backgrounds. Fifty-eight blades and twenty-two pieces of black paper were used.
Image on page 27 inspired by a photograph copyright © by Bettmann/Getty Images.
Typography by Nikki McClure and Dana Fritts
18 19 20 21 22   SCP   10 9 8 7 6 5 4 3 2 1
❖ First Edition